MAKING CENTS

by **ELIZABETH KEELER ROBINSON**

illustrations by **BOB MCMAHON**

SCHOLASTIC INC.
New York Toronto London Auckland
Sydney Mexico City New Delhi Hong Kong

Penny!

There's a pretty perfect penny in my pocket—
a copper-colored penny, very
smooth around the edge.
With this one-cent penny
we can buy . . .

a perfect
penny nail.

Look! We have five pennies.
We can trade them for a . . .

Nickel!

A shining silver nickel
bigger than a penny, with a
sleek and polished rim.
A five-cent nickel buys . . .

five perfect penny nails

or

a sharply spiraled
wood screw, either
Phillips head or flat.

If we earn two silver nickels
(or ten pretty perfect pennies),
we can take them in and trade
them up for one thin . . .

Dime!

A dinky, dainty dime—
the smallest silver coin, it has a
corrugated edge.
A ten-cent dime buys . . .

ten perfect penny nails

or

two spiraled wood screws,
either Phillips head or flat

or

a marking pencil, bold
and black, that sharpens
with a string.

If we earn two dimes and a single, silver nickel
(or five silver nickels, or twenty-five whole pennies),
we can stack them very neatly and exchange them for a . . .

Quarter!

The biggest silver coin, it has a
creased and crinkled rim.
Twenty-five cents—
that's the value of a quarter,
which I calculate will buy us . . .

twenty-five whole perfect penny nails *or*

five spiraled wood screws, either Phillips head or flat

or

two marking pencils (with a nickel back in change)

or

a scratchy square of sandpaper for smoothing splinters out.

If we have four quarters (or ten dinky, dainty dimes,
or twenty silver nickels, or a hundred perfect pennies),
we can take them to the bank
and get a crisp . . .

One-dollar bill!

There's President George Washington,
and on the back, a pyramid, an eagle, and a ONE.
It's worth one hundred cents but can be folded,
rolled, or fluttered.
A crisp paper dollar buys . . .

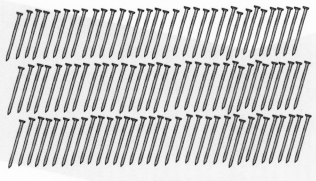

one hundred penny nails

or

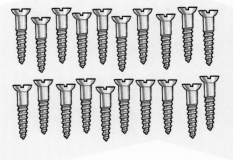

twenty spiraled wood screws

or **ten marking pencils**   *or* **four squares of sandpaper**   *or* **a sturdy hinge to make a door that opens up and closes.**

Once we make five singles,
we'll exchange them for a . . .

Five-dollar bill!

Look, Abraham Lincoln's
on the front and on the back.
Five hundred cents—
that's the value of a fiver.
A five-dollar bill will buy . . .

500 x

five hundred
penny nails

or

100 x

one hundred
wood screws

or

50 x

fifty marking
pencils

20 x

or twenty squares
of sandpaper

5 x

or five sturdy
hinges

1 x

or a shiny, yellow tape
measure, all curled
inside a case.

If we earn a pair of fivers, we can trade them for a

Ten-dollar bill!

That's Alexander Hamilton. Now flip to see the Treasury in Washington, D.C. It's worth one thousand cents and can buy . . .

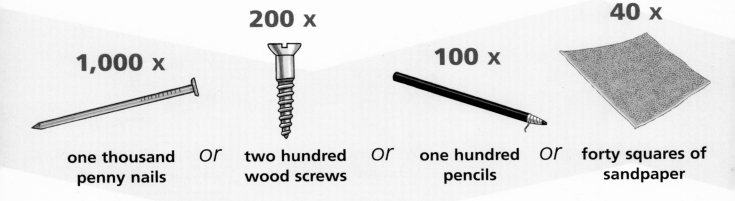

1,000 x

one thousand penny nails

or

200 x

two hundred wood screws

or

100 x

one hundred pencils

or

40 x

forty squares of sandpaper

10 x

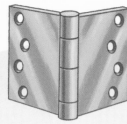

or ten sturdy hinges

2 x

or two yellow tape measures

1 x

or a level with some bubble tubes to make sure things are straight.

Soon we'll have two tens, and they'll add up to a . . .

Twenty-dollar bill!

Andrew Jackson's on the front
and that's the White House on the back.
It's worth two thousand cents,
but it's easier to carry.
That twenty-dollar bill can buy . . .

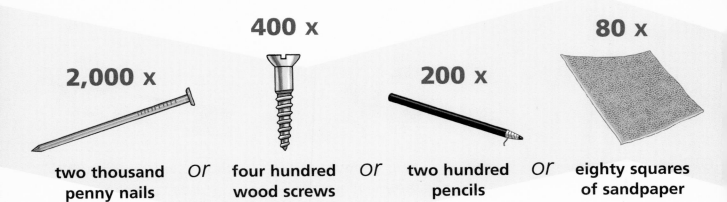

2,000 x

two thousand
penny nails

or

400 x

four hundred
wood screws

or

200 x

two hundred
pencils

or

80 x

eighty squares
of sandpaper

20 x

or **twenty sturdy hinges**

4 x

or **four yellow tape measures**

2 x

or **two bubbled levels**

1 x

or **a bucket full of house paint in a super shade of blue.**

If we earn two twenties plus another ten,
we'll trade them for a . . .

Fifty-dollar bill!

It shows the U. S. Capitol
and General U. S. Grant.
Five thousand cents
is the value of a fifty.
We can save those fifty dollars
or can buy . . .

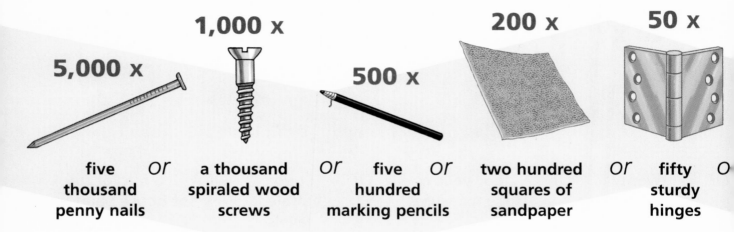

5,000 x
five
thousand
penny nails

or

1,000 x
a thousand
spiraled wood
screws

or

500 x
five
hundred
marking pencils

or

200 x
two hundred
squares of
sandpaper

or

50 x
fifty
sturdy
hinges

o

10 x

ten yellow tape
measures

or

5 x

five levels,
each with tubes

or

2 x

two buckets full
of paint (with ten
bucks back in change)

or

1 x

a folding ladder,
strong and tall,
for working way
up high.

Once we make two fifties,
we can swap them for a . . .

Hundred-dollar bill!

Wow! A hundred-dollar bill—
Ben Franklin's on the front side
backed by Independence Hall.
It's worth ten thousand cents,
which will buy . . .

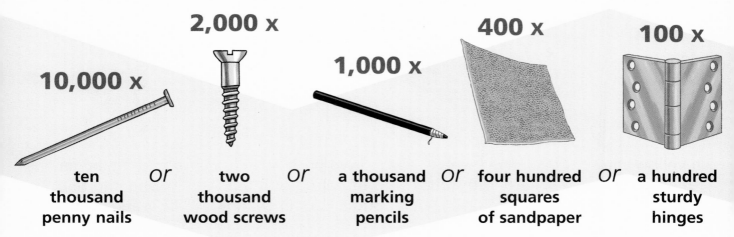

10,000 x

ten
thousand
penny nails

or

2,000 x

two
thousand
wood screws

or

1,000 x

a thousand
marking
pencils

or

400 x

four hundred
squares
of sandpaper

or

100 x

a hundred
sturdy
hinges

20 x
or twenty yellow tape measures

10 x
or ten levels, each with tubes

5 x
or five cans of house paint

2 x
or two folding ladders

or plywood sheets, some two-by-fours, a hammer, and a saw.

Hey, look at that! We did it!
We worked and planned and saved,
then we built something really great!
Let's call our friends and celebrate!

CLUBHOUSE
PARTY
TODAY!

FREE
LEMONADE

AUTHOR'S NOTE

The kids in this book sure know their way around American currency—and now you do, too. But did you know that there are also half-dollar and dollar coins and a two-dollar bill? I left them out because they're not as common as the other denominations. In fact, many vending machines won't take them—and imagine how stuffed your pockets would be if you had to carry dollar coins instead of bills!

Have you seen these less-common denominations? Here's how to tell for sure. The half-dollar coin is the biggest silver coin and has a picture of John F. Kennedy on the face. The dollar coin is gold colored and features a portrait of Sacagawea, the Shoshone woman who led Lewis and Clark when they explored the American West. (That's her son, Jean Baptiste, on her back.) The two-dollar bill—the rarest of all bills in use today—features a portrait of Thomas Jefferson.

Our money is always changing. In 2007, the U.S. Mint began issuing one-dollar coins featuring portraits of all of the presidents of the United States. Four new coins will be issued each year until the series is complete in 2016. Thomas Jefferson's portrait on the nickel has changed twice since 2003, and four different designs were used on the nickel's back between 2004 and 2006. Between 1999 and 2008, the eagle on the back side of a quarter was replaced by pictures representing the fifty states. The quarter in this book features the state of Virginia, the home state of the first U.S. president, George Washington (who is, of course, on the front of the quarter).

Keep up with these changes and learn more about American currency by visiting the websites of the Bureau of Printing and Engraving (www.moneyfactory.gov) and the U.S. Mint (www.usmint.gov).

To Julia, Emily, and Abigail,
who are priceless.
—E.K.R.

To Lalane, Tyler, and Lily
for all their kind help.
—B.M.

ISBN 978-0-545-44895-6

Text copyright © 2008 by Elizabeth Keeler Robinson.
Illustrations copyright © 2008 by Bob McMahon.
All rights reserved. Published by Scholastic Inc., 557 Broadway, New York, NY 10012, by arrangement with Tricycle Press, an imprint of Random House Children's Books, a division of Random House, Inc. SCHOLASTIC and associated logos are trademarks and/or registered trademarks of Scholastic Inc.

12 11 10 9 8 7 6 5 4   13 14 15 16 17/0

Printed in the U.S.A.   40

First Scholastic printing, February 2012

Design by Susan Van Horn
Typeset in Frutiger and Inflex Bold
The illustrations in this book were rendered in Corel Painter.